VANCOUVE...

THE CITY AT A GLA...

GW00724792

English Bay
Blending Edwardian elegan...
beach, this enclave offers hi...
saltwater, not to mention ur...

One Wall Centre
Located at Downtown's highest point, Busby
+ Associates' tower ushered in Vancouver's
metamorphosis into a 'vertical' city.
See p012

The Electra
This 1957 building, designed by Thompson
Berwick Pratt, boasts a unique, diamond-
like shape and striking interior tilework.
See p065

Robson Square
Here, Arthur Erickson and Cornelia Oberlander
created one of Canada's finest public spaces.
See p066

BC Place
This sports stadium boasts the largest air-
supported dome in the world and will host
the 2010 Winter Olympic Games ceremonies.
See p014

Stanley Park
One of the country's largest urban parks
boasts a 8.8km seawall, half a million trees,
extensive gardens and 200km of trails.

Harbour Centre Tower
Catch panoramic views from the top of this
1977 building designed by architects WZMH.
See p013

Canada Place
The graceful white sails of Expo 86's Canada
Pavilion make this a defining city landmark.
See p010

INTRODUCTION
THE CHANGING FACE OF THE URBAN SCENE

A sea of green mirrored high-rises christened the City of Glass by local author Douglas Coupland, Vancouver is a place of ephemeral beauty. Should denizens of Canada's third largest metropolis ever get homesick while on the road, quick televisual comfort can be found, as the city has played hundreds of others in countless Hollywood films. It's easy to see why. Vancouver has a cinematic skin: a lush sensuality born of the mountains that embrace it, the ocean that surrounds it and the parks and forests that make it truly green. But the celluloid city has a dark side, notably the Downtown Eastside, Canada's poorest postcode, and growing gang violence. Nevertheless, on a sunny spring day, with its streets full of cherry blossom and its multicultural citizens bursting with Olympic-inspired pride, Vancouver could double as a metropolitan paradise.

The city's set is currently under construction, with a building frenzy not seen since Expo 86. New towers vie for the title of tallest, 100 restaurants opened in 2007 alone, and entire neighbourhoods, such as Coal Harbour, have been carved out of landfill, stretching progress to its aquatic limits. From Terminal City, which was the Canadian Pacific Railway moniker for the end-of-the-line port town, to would-be urban utopia, Vancouver has come a long way since its incorporation in 1886. And the lure of Lotusland as the place to reinvent yourself remains strong, with 40 per cent of its populace born elsewhere. Could the city finally be ready for its close-up?

ESSENTIAL INFO
FACTS, FIGURES AND USEFUL ADDRESSES

TOURIST OFFICE
Vancouver Tourist Info Centre
Plaza, 200 Burrard Street
T 604 683 2000
tourismvancouver.com

TRANSPORT
Bus
T 604 953 3333
translink.bc.ca
Car hire
Avis
757 Hornby Street
T 604 606 2868
Taxis
Black Top & Checker Cabs
T 604 731 1111
blacktopcheckercabs.supersites.ca
Yellow Cab
T 604 681 1111
www.yellowcabonline.com

EMERGENCY SERVICES
Emergencies
T 911
Police (non-emergencies)
T 604 717 3321
24-hour pharmacy
Shoppers Drug Mart
1125 Davie Street
T 604 669 2424
shoppersdrugmart.ca

CONSULATES
British Consulate
1111 Melville Street
T 604 683 4421
www.britainincanada.org
US Consulate
1075 W Pender Street
T 604 685 4311
vancouver.usconsulate.gov

MONEY
American Express
Suite 103
1166 Alberni Street
T 604 669 3338
travel.americanexpress.com

POSTAL SERVICES
Post Office
349 W Georgia Street
T 800 267 1177
Shipping
FedEx
T 1800 463 3339
fedex.com/ca

BOOKS
City of Glass by Douglas Coupland
(Douglas & McIntyre)
**Seven Stones: A Portrait of Arthur
Erickson, Architect** by Edith Iglauer
(Harbour Publishing)
Vancouver Stories (Raincoast Books)

WEBSITES
Architecture
canada.archiseek.com
Newspaper
vancouversun.com

COST OF LIVING
**Taxi from Vancouver International
Airport to Downtown**
£13
Cappuccino
£1.50
Packet of cigarettes
£2.60
Daily newspaper
£0.65
Bottle of champagne
£50

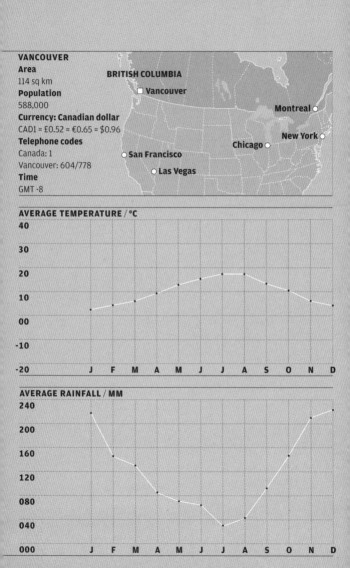

VANCOUVER
Area
114 sq km
Population
588,000
Currency: Canadian dollar
CAD1 = £0.52 = €0.65 = $0.96
Telephone codes
Canada: 1
Vancouver: 604/778
Time
GMT -8

BRITISH COLUMBIA

☐ Vancouver

Montreal ○

New York ○

Chicago ○

○ San Francisco

○ Las Vegas

AVERAGE TEMPERATURE / °C

40												
30												
20												
10												
00												
-10												
-20	J	F	M	A	M	J	J	A	S	O	N	D

AVERAGE RAINFALL / MM

240												
200												
160												
120												
080												
040												
000	J	F	M	A	M	J	J	A	S	O	N	D

NEIGHBOURHOODS
THE AREAS YOU NEED TO KNOW AND WHY

To help you navigate the city, we've chosen the most interesting districts (see below and the map inside the back cover) and colour-coded our featured venues, according to their location; those venues that are outside these areas are not coloured.

KITSILANO

This beachfront area is named after chief Khatsalano, whose people were evicted to make room for this new suburb a century ago. The area survived 1960s and 1970s hippiedom to become a sought-after 'hood, where no self-respecting bohemian could afford to live. Coconut-oil-scented summers turn Kits into Venice Beach North.

SOUTH GRANVILLE

This is Vancouver's original posh enclave, where railway barons' mansions have been acquired by telecommunications magnates, and is still the city's chicest neighbourhood. Boutiques, cafés and galleries offer *luxe, calme et volupté*.

SOUTH MAIN

At the end of the 1990s, SoMa emerged from the traditional Mount Pleasant area as the city's hipster central. Now artists are being edged out of their lofts to make way for upscale condos and some galleries are being converted into fashion boutiques. But the area remains quirky and transitional.

DOWNTOWN

Vancouver has one of North America's most densely populated downtown cores, with the shift from business to residential real estate a hallmark of the new 'Vancouverism' that has urbanists abuzz. People live, work, eat and play in a two-mile radius brimming with restaurants, retail stops and luxurious residences.

CHINATOWN

The bulk of new Chinese arrivals make their home in nearby Richmond, but Chinatown remains a museum of mainly Cantonese immigrant life, with its original architecture, night markets and wonton eateries. Steps away from the Downtown Eastside, it's already sporting new condo developments and boutiques.

WEST END

Vancouver's earliest upscale suburb became a midcentury haven for immigrants from Mitteleuropa. Robsonstraße morphed into an aggressive retail mecca in the 1980s, but Davie Street remains truly urban and the home of the city's gay village.

GASTOWN

Built on the bones of the original city, which survived the great fire of 1886, Gastown became the inspiration for the term 'skid row'. But its cobblestone streets, historic architecture and cheap rents have attracted fledgling designers, notably to 300 Block Cordova, and hot new restaurateurs.

VALETOWN

The former Canadian Pacific Railway (CPR) land was rediscovered by artists looking for cheap warehouse space and gentrified in the late 1980s, breeding high-end condos, fine dining and shops. A few new galleries and the Roundhouse Community Centre (181 Roundhouse Mews, T 604 713 1800) point to signs of a cultural revival.

LANDMARKS

THE SHAPE OF THE CITY SKYLINE

Vancouver's population is growing rapidly, and the latest planning buzzword is ecodensity, which tends to translate, in practical terms, as vertical expansion. The city's patron saint of architecture, Arthur Erickson, has designed two new towers, including The Residences at the Ritz-Carlton (1090 W Georgia Street, T 604 689 8881), while the Shangri-La (1128 W Georgia Street, T 604 689 1120) hotel and condo development, due to be finished in 2009, will strip One Wall Centre (see p012) of its highest-occupied-floor-in-town title.

The cityscape has transformed since the days when its Beaux Arts copper-domed Sun Tower (100 W Pender Street) was the tallest in the British Empire at 82m. Or when the art deco Burrard Bridge, now almost permanently congested, was more than ample for local traffic. In 1977, the Harbour Centre Tower (see p013) took the title of the city's tallest. It's still a great vantage point, and from its revolving restaurant you can see as far as Mount Baker.

On the northern Downtown shore, Canada Place (overleaf), with its iconic sail design, and the adjacent convention centre, to be completed in 2009, will welcome the Olympic community, while half a mile away, the oddly shaped BC Place (see p014) is a legacy of Expo 86, and is a humbling reminder of the excesses of event-fuelled architectural hubris. The marshmallow-like dome, which has a habit of collapsing, will be given a new roof after 2010. *For full addresses, see Resources.*

Canada Place

Vancouver's earnest cousin to Sydney's opera house is poised on the Burrard Inlet waterfront. The joint project for Expo 86, designed by architects Musson Cattell Mackey, Downs Archambault and Zeidler Roberts, transformed an old cargo pier into a city landmark: a tent-like structure with five sails of Teflon-coated fibreglass fabric suspended from 10 steel masts. The complex includes the existing Vancouver Convention & Exhibition Centre (T 604 689 8232), the Pan Pacific hotel (T 604 662 8111), Port Authority offices and the world's first IMAX theatre (T 604 682 4629). It's also the ideal place to ponder the city's past and future, its boardwalk offering glimpses of the new convention centre and industrial beauty of the wharves. *780-999 Canada Place, T 604 775 7200, canadaplace.ca*

One Wall Centre

This 150m tower of glass, designed by Busby + Associates (now Busby Perkins + Will), was completed in 2001. The building's top 17 floors of clear glazed residential units (one once occupied by action star Jean-Claude Van Damme) emerge from the lower 30 floors of darker glazed hotel and conference space. Situated between two of the city's most architecturally important buildings, Arthur Erickson's courthouse (see p066) and the former BC Hydro HQ (see p065), and opposite two neo-Gothic churches, this slim, elliptical structure ushered in Vancouver's metamorphosis into a vertical city, and has become a civic landmark visible from almost anywhere.
938 Nelson Street, T 604 688 8000

Harbour Centre Tower

When Neil Armstrong opened the Harbour Centre Tower in 1977, consumer confidence was high, and so was the building, sired by WZMH, the same architectural firm that built Toronto's CN Tower. The spire that extended the structure's height to 177m seemed straight out of *The Jetsons*. But the cast-concrete tower came crashing down to earth in the 1980s, when recession hit the traditional Downtown hard and the Sears store that had occupied part of the building and several adjacent retailers closed. Fortunately, the void was filled by Simon Fraser University (see p070), which moved here in 1989. Visitors can take the glass elevators to the 360-degree Lookout or dine at the rotating Top of Vancouver restaurant (T 604 669 2220). *555 W Hastings Street, T 604 689 0421, vancouverlookout.com*

BC Place

Canada's first domed stadium has the largest air-supported roof in the world, and will host the opening and closing ceremonies for the 2010 Winter Olympic Games. Built on the north shore of False Creek, it was designed by Vancouver's PBK Architects and opened in 1983. Its first major public event was a speech by the Queen inviting the world to Expo 86. But the current home of the BC Lions football team has been something of a white elephant. Now operated at a loss of around £720,000 a year, partly due to crippling energy bills, its dome famously deflated in January 2007 when a storm tore through it. A new roof design has yet to be confirmed. *777 Pacific Boulevard, T 604 669 2300, bcplacestadium.com*

HOTELS

WHERE TO STAY AND WHICH ROOMS TO BOOK

The city is in the midst of a pre-Olympic hotel frenzy, in which it seems everything old is new again. Grandes dames, like The Fairmont Hotel Vancouver (see p026), have been busy renovating to keep up with the bright, young boutique offerings, and a new breed of luxury residential hotel, as seen in the Shangri-La (see p009), has been born. The 1927 Hotel Georgia (801 W Georgia Street), due to reopen in 2009, plans to add an apartment tower by 2011, while nearby, the Hyatt Regency (see p024) is likely to add style-conscious travellers to its current business clientele with a slick new look. A few blocks away, the Four Seasons (791 W Georgia Street, T 604 689 9333) has spearheaded its redesign with a new lobby and swank restaurant (see p052). Straddling Downtown and tony Coal Harbour is the recently opened Loden (see p030), which offers guests a dose of contemporary West Coast chic, though if you are looking to escape the noise and bustle of Downtown altogether, you should stay at the revamped Westin Bayshore (see p019).

In the small is beautiful category, the Wedgewood Hotel (845 Hornby Street, T 604 689 7777) is popular with visiting celebs seeking laid-back, low-key luxury, while The Listel Hotel (see p022) attracts both creative and business types. Over in Yaletown, the Opus Hotel (overleaf) remains the city's trendy boutique option, but may soon be outdone by the Moda Hotel (opposite). *For full addresses and room rates, see Resources.*

Dear Reader, books by Phaidon are recognized worldwide for their beauty, scholarship and elegance. We invite you to return this card with your name and e-mail address so that we can keep you informed of our new publications, special offers and events. Alternatively, visit us at **www.phaidon.com** to see our entire list of books, videos and stationery. Register on-line to be included on our regular e-newsletters.

Subjects in which I have a special interest

☐ General Non-Fiction   ☐ Art   ☐ Photography   ☐ Architecture   ☐ Design

☐ Fashion   ☐ Music   ☐ Children's   ☐ Food   ☐ Travel

Mr/Miss/Ms   Initial   Surname

Name

No./Street

City   Country

Postcode/Zip code

E-mail

This is not an order form. To order please contact Customer Services at the appropriate address overleaf.

Please delete address not required before mailing

PHAIDON PRESS INC.
180 Varick Street
New York
NY 10014
USA

PHAIDON PRESS LIMITED
Regent's Wharf
All Saints Street
London N1 9PA
UK

Return address for USA and Canada only

Return address for UK and countries outside the USA and Canada only

Affix stamp here

Moda Hotel

The antithesis of the bland, corporate hotel, this 100-year-old building has had a colourful past as an Edwardian gentlemen's drinking spot, and later as a gay cabaret, where men were men and so were the women. Its newest incarnation, a boutique hotel designed by Vancouver's Alda Pereira, boasts a striking reception, with original mosaic flooring, a black marble counter and 1908 lift, as well as textured wallpaper. Pared-down styling and exposed pipes give the rooms, such as the Deluxe King Suite 427 (above), an atelier feel, offset by beds with umpteen-thread-count linen. With its charcuterie bar, Uva (see p040), and an Italian eaterie on the way, Moda has become a foodie destination too. *900 Seymour Street, T 604 683 4251, modahotel.ca*

Opus Hotel

Although it burst onto the scene back in 2002 as the city's most stylish boutique hotel, the Opus still holds its own. Rooms are designed along five 'personality' themes, including 'Billy' – apparently a London rock star who favours lime interiors and glass doors. For LA-style detailing, reserve the Opus Penthouse (above) – a favourite of Demi Moore – done out in ruby, taupe and faux fur, and featuring a wraparound balcony and tub with a view. A personal shopper, dog walker and the use of a BMW or a Jorg & Olif bike are among the services provided for guests. The in-house bistro Elixir (T 604 642 0557) serves an appetising menu of well-executed modern French fare, while the lobby Opus Bar (T 604 642 0557) is a popular nightspot. *322 Davie Street, T 604 642 6787, opushotel.com*

The Westin Bayshore

Opened in 1961, this waterfront hotel was once secluded enough to attract the likes of Howard Hughes, who rented the top two floors in 1972. Now a Starwood property, it is surrounded by high-end condos, but thanks to its marina and views of Stanley Park and the North Shore mountains, it still feels resort-like. The interiors, by Chicago's Anderson/Miller, include soothing earth tones and handsome hardwoods. Guests seeking contemporary surrounds and lots of space should opt for the International Suite (above and overleaf), which has ash floors and Ralph Lauren furnishings; those in search of old-school luxe should book the top-floor Howard Hughes Suite, complete with soaring ceilings and a marble foyer. *1601 Bayshore Drive, T 604 682 3377, westinbayshore.com*

The Listel Hotel

This might well be the perfect Vancouver hotel. Just the right size at 129 rooms, The Listel is an aesthetic delight. Two Gallery Floors are curated by Buschlen Mowatt Galleries, and include original works by local and international artists, while the Museum Floors feature contemporary First Nations art supplied by the Museum of Anthropology (see p035). The interiors of the Museum Floor rooms (above) evoke a powerful sense of place by celebrating the muted colours of Vancouver's natural environment, while local materials appear in custom-made hemlock and cedarwood furniture. A selection of cultural magazines is offered to guests, including the local literary title *Geist*. O'Doul's Restaurant & Bar, located off the lobby (right), serves up jazz and fine seafood.
1300 Robson Street, T 604 684 8461, thelistelhotel.com

Hyatt Regency

When this hotel launched in 1973, it was one of the tallest buildings in town, and with its glass elevator and rooftop disco Odyssey, represented the height of 1970s sophistication. The elevator met a sorry fate in the 80s, when during the filming of TV cop show *MacGyver*, it was accidentally blown up, and Vancouver's answer to Studio 54 is now reserved for the corporate hustle. A 2007 redesign – a sleek scheme using wood, glass, steel and stone – by local firm MCM Interiors has boosted this business hotel's hip factor. Maximising natural light and views was key in the remodelling of the spacious rooms, such as the Signature Suite 3304 (above and right). Its black, grey and red palette and Eero Saarinen's 'Womb' chairs for Knoll should entice design aficionados, as well as modern-day disco queens.
655 Burrard Street, T 604 683 1234, vancouver.hyatt.com

The Fairmont Hotel Vancouver

The venerable 17-storey 'Hotel Van', as it's often referred to by locals, was opened by George VI and Queen Elizabeth in 1939 and remains a city landmark, with its distinctive oxidised copper roof, Gothic-style gargoyles and interiors laden with mahogany, brass and crystal. Period elegance is preserved in the soft-hued Gold Loggia Suites (above), which each feature an enclosed parlour-cum-balcony with sweeping views. Up-to-the-minute comfort can be found in the Absolute Spa, while the past shines through in the nickel-trimmed art moderne elevator foyer in the lower lobby, which has a marble-chipped terrazzo floor. The lounge off the main lobby (right), which is due to be revamped by the LA-based Virginia Ball, is the location of nightly jazz sets and an ideal place to hold court.
900 W Georgia Street, T 604 684 3131, fairmont.com/hotelvancouver

Pacific Palisades

This 1968 West End hotel tower began life as a Shangri-La, but was taken over by the Kimpton group in 2000 and given a Cheryl Rowley, Miami-style redesign. It's a long way from South Beach, but on a grey Vancouver day, the bursts of colour in the rooms and public spaces are a breath of fresh air. The Rouge Over Robson Penthouse Suite (above and left), with its mod furnishings and lipstick-red scheme, is guaranteed to banish SAD. The hotel is also a mildly camp fantasy, from the indoor poolside cabana to the mirror-mosaic wall art by bellman Ken Armich – just right for the Hollywood North types who often stay here. An on-site art gallery and the Zin Restaurant & Lounge provide aesthetic distraction and culinary pleasure. *1277 Robson Street, T 604 688 0461, pacificpalisadeshotel.com*

Loden
Designed by local firm Hewitt + Kwasnicky
Architects, this 14-storey glass, stone
and copper hotel tower was inspired
by the city's aquatic environment.
The snug, caramel, coral and chocolate
interiors, as seen in the Deluxe King
(pictured) and the 148 sq m penthouse,
were created by San Francisco's BAMO.
1177 Melville Street, T 604 669 5060,
lodenvancouver.com

24 HOURS

SEE THE BEST OF THE CITY IN JUST ONE DAY

Vancouver's stunning natural backdrop, its burgeoning visual-arts culture and its growing foodie scene mean you can experience a happy harmony of the outdoors, the aesthetically pleasing and the appetising in one well-planned day. If the weather's fine, you might want to travel by bicycle or bus, as distances are not huge, but traffic snarls will inevitably slow you down.

Breakfast at Granville Island (opposite), on the south shore of False Creek, before touring the artisanal studios there. Then begin your art tour, with a little nature thrown in, by heading to the city's westernmost peninsula, where The University of British Columbia offers Arthur Erickson's Museum of Anthropology (overleaf) and the Morris and Helen Belkin Art Gallery. For a more urban art experience, head next to the Monte Clark Gallery (see p037) and, if there's time, the Bill Reid Gallery (639 Hornby Street, T 604 682 3455), which is a block away from the venerable Vancouver Art Gallery (750 Hornby Street, T 604 879 4719).

No trip to Vancouver would be complete without a mosey round Stanley Park, where you can stop for lunch at Raincity Grill (see p036). Then make for Chinatown, the second largest in North America, where you'll find much intact heritage architecture. End the day with a walk along Kits Beach and dinner at Watermark (see p038), whose architectural élan nearly trumps the view. *For full addresses, see Resources.*

08.00 Granville Island

This former industrial area was converted in the late 1970s into one of Vancouver's most successful public spaces. There's lots here, including a food market, the Emily Carr University (T 604 844 3800) – alma mater of Douglas Coupland and home of the Charles H Scott Gallery (T 604 844 3809) – as well as shops and design studios. Granville Island also boasts a marina, in the Sea Village community, and one of the finest modernist houseboats you'll ever see. After perking yourself up with some coffee and an almond croissant from La Baguette et L'Echalote (T 604 684 1351), check out the jewellery at Object Design (T 604 683 7763); the wearable art and edgy ceramics at Funk Shui Atelier (T 604 684 5327); and the work of up-and-coming glass artists at New-Small & Sterling (T 604 681 6730).

11.00 Museum of Anthropology

This is the perfect pilgrimage for Arthur Erickson groupies and fans of First Nations art. Erickson's 1976 building (above) – a cliff-top modernist concrete riff on traditional north-west coast post-and-beam architecture – features soaring glass walls that overlook the mountains and sea. Highlights of the collection include totem poles and carved boxes, which are displayed in the Great Hall.

The largest teaching museum in Canada is currently undergoing a £26.5m renovation, which will expand it by 50 per cent by 2009. Close by, at the Morris and Helen Belkin Art Gallery (left; T 604 822 2759), designed by Peter Cardew Architects, the emphasis is on emerging artists and the Canadian avant-garde of the 1960s and 1970s. *6393 NW Marine Drive, T 604 822 3825, moa.ubc.ca*

14.00 Raincity Grill

A pioneer of the locavore movement, which uses ingredients sourced within a 100-mile radius, the elegant Raincity Grill, owned by local restaurateur Harry Kambolis, who also runs Nu (T 604 646 4668) and C (T 604 681 1164), offers stunning views of English Bay to accompany its excellent tasting menu. Dominic Ratte's understated oak and earth-toned interior lets the food speak louder than the design and provides a light and airy setting for lunch. Try the butternut squash soup with hazelnut, then the Saltspring Island mussels with chorizo, tomato, white wine and Yukon Gold potato chips, paired with a local BC wine, such as Blue Mountain Brut. If it's a sunny day, try to reserve a seat on the patio.
1193 Denman Street, T 604 685 7337, raincitygrill.com

16.00 Monte Clark Gallery

In a city famed for its photoconceptualism, this gallery is a natural choice. It represents second- and third-generation Vancouver School photographers, who are known for their intensity and distanced yet socially conscious gaze. Artists such as the internationally respected Roy Arden and Karen Bubas have shown here, as has Renaissance man Douglas Coupland, whose exhibit, *Spike*, explored issues of environmental toxicity via stylised toy soldiers with deformed limbs. But the gallery also exhibits up-and-comers and is often touted as *the* place to discover the next big thing. It's certainly the place with the best opening parties.
2339 Granville Street, T 604 730 5000, www.monteclarkgallery.com

20.00 Watermark

Architect Tony Robins had to defend his vision for a modernist restaurant on Kitsilano Beach all the way to the BC Supreme Court. Incorporating a 1965 Parks Board concession stand and lifeguard station, the 2005 Watermark, all steel, glass and concrete, hits high notes design- and cuisine-wise. Its upper-level restaurant, inspired by Pierre Chareau's Maison de Verre in Paris, Japanese proportions and a priceless view, serves up West Coast seafood and Asian-influenced fare, and is the perfect blend of natural and architectural beauty. Bolted steel columns referencing the freighters in the harbour are softened by stained oak flooring and cedar panels. When sunset colours stream in, the lobster risotto tastes even better. *1305 Arbutus Street, T 604 738 5487, watermarkrestaurant.ca*

22.00 George

This cocktail lounge with an interior by Mitchell Friedland is a good spot in which to rev up for a big night. The crowd — a mix of visiting supermodels, film stars, locals and Yaletown fashionistas — vies for attention with the design: West Coast minimalism has been banished in favour of a rich palette of luxe materials. Comfy yet elegant banquettes beckon with their burgundy velvet and black leather.

A wraparound bar made of translucent Brazilian onyx, with a multi-hued Dale Chihuly-esque glass installation overhead, provides a good perch from which to enjoy the resident DJ's tunes or sip a cocktail. If you come here again, the upstairs restaurant Brix (T 604 915 9463) serves up delicious West Coast/Continental plates. *1137 Hamilton Street, T 604 628 5555, georgelounge.com*

URBAN LIFE
CAFÉS, RESTAURANTS, BARS AND NIGHTCLUBS

The city's restaurant scene has exploded in the last few years. As rents rise and foodie intrigue has become the new celebrity gossip, the competition can only get hotter. The other thing everyone loves to talk about here is the locavore trend, which has become such an obsession that top eateries, such as Blue Water Café + Raw Bar (see p054), are now celebrated as much for their local, sustainable ingredients as the quality of their cooking. And the look is fresh too. With the likes of local firm Evoke shaping restaurants such as Habit (see p050) and Coast (see p048), some of Vancouver's best contemporary interior design is to be found in its dining rooms.

It is hard to beat this city for the sheer variety and bargain prices of its cuisine. Vancouver's Asian eateries are among the best in North America, from hole-in-the-wall ramen houses to the celebrated Indian restaurant Vij's (see p060). And now that many bars and clubs are open until 3am, you can dance off your dinner around town. For a sophisticated evening out, the current craze for cocktails can be experienced at the likes of George (see p039), while Downtown's Uva (900 Seymour Street, T 604 632 9560) is a great example of the growing trend towards charcuteries where meats are expertly paired with wines. More bohemian tastes can be cultivated at The Cellar Jazz Club (see p061) and at Havana (see p046), which is restaurant, bar, gallery and theatre all in one. *For full addresses, see Resources.*

Tojo's

When owner/chef Hidekazu Tojo came to Vancouver in the early 1970s, he hoped that its open, multicultural vibe would make the city the ideal venue for his growing taste for culinary experimentation. Luckily he was right, and his inventions – the inside-out California roll and the barbecued salmon-skin BC roll – became classics. Tojo's speciality is its *omakase*: a kind of spontaneous dégustation menu, taking into consideration the diner's preferences and the chef's fancy. In 2007, Tojo's moved to a space designed by Azurean Architecture, with a curved ceiling inspired by Shinto shrines, a palette of white and blue/grey, and Zen-like elements of wood, stone, water and greenery – all of which enhance the dining experience. *1133 W Broadway, T 604 872 8050, tojos.com*

Gastropod

Scott Cohen's sleek, understated design, using salvaged midcentury oak and fir and a mint and slate colour scheme, complements chef Angus An's sublime menu, both featuring simple elements blended with élan. An, who previously worked at what is currently the world's only Michelin-starred Thai restaurant, Nahm, in London, offers Asian- and French-themed creations that are more alchemy than fusion. In his dishes he focuses on a few strong ingredients at a time, reinterpreting classics while maintaining their original integrity. The results are heavenly; for instance, the almost ephemeral oysters with horseradish snow, and organic lamb with saffron béarnaise.
1938 W 4th Avenue, T 604 730 5579, gastropod.ca

Epicurean Caffè

On a sunny day in Kitsilano, you can squint a little and pretend you're in Italy, especially if you're sitting on the terrace of the Epicurean Caffè, surrounded by fig trees and the intoxicating aroma of espresso. It has held its own since 1993, serving excellent coffees, decadent pastries and bistro-style lunch and dinner dishes in a cosy yet elegant interior of Carrara marble, glass and mahogany.

But the real attraction here is the lovely Cocco family: the radiant Renata, *la mamma* who still prepares most of the delicious, traditional cuisine, such as *gnocchi all'amatriciana*, and her handsome son, Christian, who manages the café and the upstairs private function space, Epic Lounge (T 604 733 5228). *1898 W 1st Avenue, T 604 731 5370, www.epicureancaffe.com*

Salt Tasting Room
If you find yourself craving Cornish Yarg
one rainy day, fear not. There's more to
this town than locavore fish and greens.
A pioneer in the charcuterie trend,
Gastown's Salt Tasting Room, located in
an old warehouse, upgraded with spruce
benches and Philippe Starck stools,
offers exquisite cheese, meats and wines.
45 Blood Alley, T 604 633 1912,
salttastingroom.com

Havana

This venue has occupied a unique space in the city's cultural landscape for more than a decade and is located at the heart of the Commerical Drive neighbourhood, an area accommodating fashionable lefties, yuppies with condos, the vestiges of Italian immigrant life and a new Latino population. Havana manages to cover all these bases, with its patio where hipsters sip mojitos or Latin American wines; its Cuban-inspired Nuevo Latino cuisine; and edgy art and theatre. The interiors, conceived by a film-set designer, evoke a stylised version of pre-revolutionary Havana, with maroon booths, vintage ceiling fans and a salvaged-steel bar. *1212 Commercial Drive, T 604 253 9119, havana-art.com*

Cobre

Vancouver may be a cold and wet 3,200-odd kilometres from the Mexican border, but its Latino community continues to grow, as does the local appetite for Central and South American food. Enter Cobre, which combines flavours from Argentina, Cuba, Mexico and Brazil in small plates using local ingredients. Andean lamb *pupusa* with coconut *kion chili pasilla*, and BC red snapper ceviche with *arbol chili wax bean escabech*e are among the mouthwatering dishes on offer. Designed by David Christopher, the dining room has a warm, heritage atmosphere, with exposed bricks and a striking curved copper ceiling delineating the open kitchen. The Wine Vault, with original travertine flooring, is strong on Chilean and Argentine *vino*. *52 Powell Street, T 604 669 2396, cobrerestaurant.com*

Coast

In this sophisticated seafood restaurant, the luscious blondwood panelling and understated design by David Nicolay of Evoke manages to be open and airy, but also warm and intimate. The communal table in the centre alternates as a group booking area and a place for singles to mingle, while the upstairs lounge and bar provide a more private experience. With its 'Catch Cook Eat' slogan, Coast transcends locavore earnestness to serve up seafood from all over the world. Watching talented chef Josh Wolfe prepare dishes such as lobster corndog or Jamaican jerk-spiced calamari via the open kitchen is almost as enjoyable as actually eating them. *1257 Hamilton Street, T 604 685 5010, coastrestaurant.ca*

Six Acres

Named after the acreage of the city's first settlement, this resto/lounge/bar pays homage to the original spirit of Gastown in more ways than one. Located in the Alhambra Hotel, the oldest brick building in the city, Six Acres' casual global menu and young, multicultural, boho crowd wouldn't have been so out of place in 1867. The new Gastown adventurers just drink and fight a bit less, and are partial to designer lofts. Six Acres' exposed brick walls, restored oak flooring and amber glass light fixtures, and cosy yet cool vibe, make it just the right spot for sharing plates of Italian charcuterie and antipasti or the popular gorgonzola hot pot, accompanied by BC micro-brews such as Granville Island Pale Ale.

Alhambra Hotel, 203 Carrall Street,
T 604 488 0110, sixacres.ca

Habit
David Nicolay's interior seems inspired
equally by Douglas Coupland's *Souvenir of
Canada* retro-kitsch (stylised deer heads),
the 1970s and clean, contemporary
chic. The understated menu travels the
globe but still makes you and your wallet
feel at home. Try the delicious curried
mussels steamed in coconut broth.
*2610 Main Street, T 604 877 8582,
www.habitlounge.ca*

Yew

Who would have thought that the fuddy-duddy Four Seasons (see p016) would deliver one of the city's most exciting restaurant/lounges? With New York chef Rafael Gonzalez at the helm, Yew serves a top-notch menu of West Coast classics with an international twist; try the cedar-smoked sablefish. The interior design is impressive too: San Francisco's Jennifer Johannson has created 12m-high ceilings, large windows and skylights, and used a subtle interplay of cedar, alder, walnut and elm. The floor-to-ceiling sandstone fireplace is an attractive complement to an order of champagne and oysters in the lounge, while the private dining room (above) looks onto the open wine cellar. Live Latin jazz hots up Sunday brunch. *791 W Georgia Street, T 604 692 4939, fourseasons.com/vancouver/dining*

Aurora Bistro

Thanks to its rigorously regional cuisine and design by Duncan MacCallum, Aurora Bistro was hipster central when it opened its doors in 2003. It remains noteworthy, and chef Jeff Van Geest has built up close relationships with local suppliers and growers, including a wild-mushroom forager. The seasonal menu – look out for the tea-smoked Polderside duck with truffle-marinated Okanagan goat's cheese and Hazelmere Farm beets – is as sleek and well judged as the interior design. The space has a retro cabin feel with restored fir flooring and fir panels along one wall. Aurora also boasts one of Vancouver's most extensive BC wine lists and is open for lunch and dinner weekdays and for weekend brunch.
2420 Main Street, T 604 873 9944, aurorabistro.ca

Blue Water Cafe + Raw Bar

This eaterie offers a winning combination of sustainable seafood, masterful wine pairings and sublime sushi. The late Werner Forster's design for the converted warehouse is tastefully underplayed. But the new brick and fir post-and-beam wine room, designed by Marc Bricault to hold more than 1,500 bottles in a glass-enclosed walk-in vault, is a stunner, featuring wave-like translucent blue panels hanging from the ceiling. The dining room offers enticing views of the cherrywood raw bar, with its dropped mirrored ceiling and open kitchen, where Yoshihiro Tabo prepares some of the city's best sashimi. Andrea Vescovi's wine and sake pairings are spot on and intoxicating. In spring and summer, sit outside on the heated patio.
1095 Hamilton Street, T 604 688 8078, bluewatercafe.net

West

In the long-running battle for the title of Vancouver's best restaurant, South Granville's West has fought admirably against Kitsilano's Lumière (T 604 739 8185) for years. Now that they both have new chefs, things are getting interesting. Warren Geraghty of London's L'Escargot has replaced David Hawksworth at West, and local foodies will be sure to take notes on how Geraghty's cuisine compares to Dale MacKay's at Lumière. Rumour has it that Geraghty's pasta dishes are a strong point, but West's focus on a classical French menu with West Coast elements remains the same. Werner Forster's design is as chic as ever, from the concrete exterior to the intimate interior, with its marble flooring and mirrored ceiling sculptures. *2881 Granville Street, T 604 738 8938, westrestaurant.com*

The Pear Tree

There are two reasons to drive to Burnaby – to make a pilgrimage to Arthur Erickson's Simon Fraser University (see p070) and to dine at The Pear Tree. Chef/owner Scott Jaeger and his wife Stephanie have created a fine-dining haven a half hour's drive from Downtown. Signature dishes (think classics with a twist, like flamed gin tomato soup with whipped chive cream and braised lamb shank topped with seared scallops with roasted pear risotto) are augmented by a seasonal *table d'hôte*. The design, by Situ's David Hepworth, will make you think you're still within city limits, from the charcoal porcelain-tile and frosted-glass exterior to the lacquered ebony and golden oak bar area (above). A 1,400-bottle cellar offers a list of fine BC and international wines.

4120 E Hastings Street, T 604 299 2772

Le Marrakech

When Le Marrakech opened, there was a huge untapped market of couscous-eaters eagerly awaiting a table. It satisfied the demand for an authentic Moroccan experience, from the décor of traditional lanterns and inlaid tables to the pre-meal rosewater hand-washing ritual, and delectable tagines. Slate flooring, stylised iron light fixtures and exposed ceiling beams offer some contemporary counterpoint. Traditional favourites, such as Fez salads of grilled peppers, roasted aubergine or tomato and cucumber, are bolstered by French-influenced fare, such as pan-seared lingcod. Great service, a fabulous belly dancer and a weekend DJ spinning the latest raï tunes make this an exhilarating escape without leaving town. *52 Alexander Street, T 604 688 3714, lemarrakech.ca*

Sanafir

This restaurant is named after a Sinai Peninsula town in owner Emad Yacoub's native Egypt that was part of the old Silk Road trading route. The town's innate mix of Asian, North African and Middle Eastern flavours is reflected in Sanafir's menu, which presents deceptively simple dishes, such as 'lamb', 'chicken', 'prawn' or 'vegetarian', prepared in three different culinary styles: Asian, Indian and Middle Eastern/Mediterranean. The décor, designed by Evoke, is a subtle yet striking combination of Egyptian lamps, grille work, Chinese silks, polished concrete floors and lofty ceilings, which all add to the exotic look and ambience. Head to Sanafir's upstairs lounge to sip cocktails on luxe silk-covered daybeds.
1026 Granville Street, T 604 678 1049, sanafir.ca

Republic

After the boom of the 1980s post-punk/ New Wave scene, Vancouver suffered a somnambulant decade or two. The recent revitalisation of Granville Mall – a once-derelict, 1970s failed urban-renewal project – into an arts and entertainment district, which began in earnest in 2002, has been somewhat of a success. Venues such as this one offer you a chance to mingle with ageing rock stars up from

LA, club kids and cocktail-quaffing thirtysomethings, who groove to DJs or local funk bands until 3am. If you still care about interiors that early in the morning, the space is decked out in sealed concrete, glass and steel, with a wraparound bar, travertine-tile floor and 1958 Gino Sarfatti chandeliers.
958 Granville Street, T 604 669 3266, donnellynightclubs.ca

Vij's

Vikram Vij's ode to modern Indian cuisine has been an international darling since it opened in 1994. The exquisite interior, by Vancouver's Marc Bricault, is a muted palette, lifted by laser-cut copper-plated steel lamps and subtle subcontinental references, rather than the traditional pink-silk and Ganesh-statue approach. Here, patrons can savour dishes such as the famous wine-marinated lamb popsicles in fenugreek cream curry, or *saag paneer* with Punjabi lentils and chapati. Since Vij's takes no reservations, the lounge with teak walls and amber-cushioned benches offers a chic yet cosy place to wait, while enjoying a selection of European wines or Indian and Scottish ales and ciders, and some complimentary Indian snacks.
1480 W 11th Avenue, T 604 736 6664, vijs.ca

The Cellar Restaurant/Jazz Club

This is a premier jazz venue, with performers such as tenor saxophonist David 'Fathead' Newman and Vancouver's own Brad Turner, on trumpet and piano. It is located in a low-key residential area of Kitsilano, but down the stairs you'll find a boho scene, hardwood floors, long wooden tables, soft lighting and photos of jazz greats adorning the warm red walls. This is a serious music venue, with a strict noise policy (no cell phones or chit-chat during performances) and even a weekly classical gig. Don't overlook the much-improved West Coast/Med-inspired tapas menu and growing wine and cocktail list. *3611 W Broadway, T 604 738 1959, cellarjazz.com*

INSIDER'S GUIDE

JANE COX, CREATIVE DIRECTOR

The co-founder and creative director of Cause + Affect Design (301-321 Water Street, T 604 608 1366), Jane Cox was formerly based in London, but moved back to her hometown in 2006, where she lives in Mount Pleasant and works at her office in Gastown. She likes to start the day at <u>Finch's Tea & Coffee House</u> (353 W Pender Street, T 604 899 4040). 'Everything here is top quality,' she says. 'It even serves egg and soldiers.' Cox's favourite view of the city is from a window seat at <u>Six Acres</u> (see p049), her hot tip for lunch.

The women's fashion boutiques <u>One of a Few</u> and <u>Two of a Few</u> (see p072) are 'great for finding unique pieces'. At <u>Inform Interiors</u> (see p080), Cox likes to check out the modern furniture or browse the design books, and she's also a fan of the Vancouver shoe designer <u>John Fluevog</u> (see p084). In quirky SoMa, <u>Lark</u> (see p073) is her favourite unisex boutique, and round the corner is 'the perfect coffee spot', <u>Soma</u> (151 E 8th Avenue, T 604 630 7502).

Her ideal afternoon would take in a cycle ride round Stanley Park, before a drink at <u>Parkside</u> (1906 Haro Street, T 604 683 6912). She also likes to take time out in <u>Robson Square</u> (see p066) or at the patio café in the <u>Vancouver Art Gallery</u> (750 Hornby Street, T 604 662 4719) in summer. <u>Habit</u> (see p050) is a 'popular, casual place to share a meal with friends', while <u>Chambar</u> (562 Beatty Street, T 604 879 7119) is her top choice for 'a buzzy late dinner'. *For full addresses, see Resources.*

ARCHITOUR
A GUIDE TO VANCOUVER'S ICONIC BUILDINGS

It's almost embarrassing that the most notable examples of public architecture in the city were designed by the octogenarian Arthur Erickson. Robson Square (overleaf) is one of his most successful urban projects, while the MacMillan Bloedel Building (see p068) and Simon Fraser University (see p070) are modernist classics.

Though Bing Thom's Sunset Community Centre (see p090) and Chan Centre for the Performing Arts (6265 Crescent Road, T 604 822 9197) stand out on the city's fringes, as does Richard Henriquez's BC Cancer Research Centre at 675 W 10th Avenue, and local firms like Battersby Howat and LWPAC are making their mark in residential design, visitors may be forgiven for thinking there's a city-wide cult preventing young architects from building an enduring legacy.

Erickson did have time on his side. Mid-20th-century Vancouver was a city full of civic confidence, in contrast to the less buoyant 1970s and 1980s, when it looked to Toronto and New York for its architectural models, and suffocating by-laws began to hamper new building. Now, however, there's an upswing in mood, as urbanists flock here to absorb the trend dubbed Vancouverism: the creation of a high-density, highway-free, residential core. From a planning point of view, the new model is daring, and has made Vancouver a unique urban experiment, though some critics are less than thrilled by the safe, often suburban architectural styles employed. *For full addresses, see Resources.*

The Electra

The former HQ of electricity company BC Hydro marked the pinnacle of Vancouver's postwar optimism. Mirroring the shape of the company's corporate logo, this elegant structure, with its aluminium fins encased in frosted glass, also offered up the best of BC modernism. Designed in 1957 by Thompson Berwick Pratt, it signalled the move westward of the old Downtown, from the Main and Hastings area towards the mainly residential West End. In 1993, it was converted into apartments by local firm Merrick Architecture, who added a new curtain wall, and renamed it The Electra. The squared-off lozenge form of the old BC Hydro logo is also referenced in the mosaic tilework by renowned Vancouver artist and designer BC Binning.

970 Burrard Street

Robson Square

When the first design for Robson Square, a 55-storey high-rise, was rejected, Arthur Erickson suggested turning the model on its side and extending the government complex by three city blocks. The result, completed between 1979 and 1983, and including an Edwardian courthouse turned into Vancouver Art Gallery, was a striking urban oasis. Featuring lush landscaping, including a series of ponds and waterfalls, designed by Cornelia Oberlander, it offers a contemplative green space in Downtown's heart. The interior of the Provincial Law Courts (left) reveals the further intermarriage of green and urban elements, with ivy creeping over the concrete terraces that act as visual counterpoint to the zigzagging structures supporting the sloping glass roof.
800 Robson Street, T 604 822 3333

MacMillan Bloedel Building

While Erickson's residential design classic Graham House was recently knocked down when it fell through heritage law cracks, and one of his office buildings, the Evergreen (1285 W Pender Street), was narrowly saved from demolition, the architect's 1965 MacMillan Bloedel Building stands proud. This exquisitely executed modernist structure, comprising two 27-floor towers set around a central core, was designed in collaboration with Geoffrey Massey, as the HQ for Canadian forestry giant MacMillan Bloedel, since sold to US company Weyerhaeuser. Nicknamed the 'concrete waffle', the building features a column-free interior and an exterior constructed of textured cast-in-place concrete. Flared like a trunk at the base, it evokes the presence of an ancient tree. *1075 W Georgia Street*

Marine Building

One of the world's great art deco towers, the Marine Building, completed in 1930, was the brainchild of entrepreneur JW Hobbs, who envisioned a Gotham-style skyscraper to put a post-Panama-Canal Vancouver on the international shipping map. Its creators, architects McCarter Nairne & Partners, were given relatively free rein and a generous budget, with impressive results. The exterior and interior feature floral and faunal motifs, such as the stylised sea creatures in the lobby, while ships and speeding trains depict Vancouver's rapid progress. The entrance pays tribute to Captain George Vancouver, his ship set against a rising sun. After the 1929 Wall Street crash, the 22-storey building was bought by the Guinness family for a bargain £445,000.
355 Burrard Street, T 604 683 8604

Simon Fraser University (SFU)

Opened in 1965, and often demonised by locals for being too radical (in its politics) and austere (in its design), the SFU campus, set on Burnaby mountain, is an enduring modernist vision. Designed by a young Arthur Erickson and Geoffrey Massey, it is a masterful expression of Erickson's 'concrete is the marble of our time' ethos. Following a processional path from the mountain's eastern summit to its western edge, and inspired by the sacred origins of the university, such as Cairo's El Azhar mosque, the campus was conceived as a series of open terraces extending down the mountainside. Highlights include a Moghul-inspired pond, mosaic murals on the concrete pillars, the rotunda library and the open-plan plaza area – the site of many student protests in the 1960s. *8888 University Drive, T 778 782 3111*

SHOPPING

THE BEST RETAIL THERAPY AND WHAT TO BUY

Boosted by the emergence of Gastown as a creative hot zone, the city's retail scene is flourishing. The bygone glamour of Downtown shopping, traditionally centred on malls and department stores such as The Bay (674 Granville Street, T 604 681 6211), is gradually returning and epitomised by Holt Renfrew (737 Dunsmuir Street, T 604 681 3121). Revamped by New York-based architect Janson Goldstein, the store now boasts three gleaming floors of luxe offerings and a 111-piece glass installation by local designer Omer Arbel. Nearby, the multilingual Sophia Books (450 W Hastings Street, T 604 684 0484) has an excellent range of design titles.

Edgy boutiques such as Obakki (see p086) are sprouting up like mushrooms in Gastown. Here you'll also find Inform Interiors (see p080) and John Fluevog (see p084). For whimsical fashion, check out One of a Few (354 Water Street, T 604 605 0685), which stocks a well-edited mix of local labels – Ashley Watson, Isabelle Dunlop, Imaginary Friend, Souvenir and Lisbeth; its next-door store, Two of a Few (T 604 605 0630), offers menswear and shoes.

Chinatown's emporiums have been joined by the chic Peking Lounge (see p082), while the traditional antiques hunting ground of SoMa is now home to fashion stop-offs like Lark (opposite). If you need a boost, a pitstop at Picnic Café (see p078) could make for an encounter with some dangerously delicious brownies. *For full addresses, see Resources.*

Lark

Located in one of Vancouver's oldest neighbourhoods, Lark embodies the area's sea change, its window display of local and European fashion facing the old Mount Pleasant clock and a new condo development. The mix of elegant yet down-to-earth pieces here represents both shiny new Vancouver and its boho West Coast roots. From the Zeha Berlin footwear to goatskin bags by the locally based Tannis Hegan, lines soon blur into one singular experience of chic. Husband-and-wife duo Dane Baspaly, a set designer, and Veronika, a painter, converted the 185 sq m space, which was formerly the Aion gallery, now located a few blocks away. *2315 Main Street, T 604 879 5275, lark8thave.com*

Martha Sturdy
Internationally renowned Vancouver
designer Martha Sturdy is constantly
pushing the boundaries – whether
it's jewellery, furniture, sculpture or
accessories, her trademark is a unique
fusion of art and design. Her clean, bold
pieces were once available in South
Granville, but in 2006, Sturdy decamped
to the 5th and Main area and set up a new
studio/gallery retail location. Open
weekdays from 10am to 4pm, it offers
creations such as her 3D resin and steel
sculptures, her signature resin floating
tables, 1.8m steel plates and paintings
on steel canvases. Sturdy's work is often
large and dramatic yet sophisticated
and minimalist. It's not difficult to
see why Donna Karan was smitten and
invited her to exhibit at her former
London flagship on New Bond Street.
16 W 5th Avenue, T 604 872 5205,
marthasturdy.com

Hunt and Gather
Fashion is presented as functional art in this atelier/boutique. The daughter of a Japanese mother and German father, designer Natalie Purschwitz studied art and archaeology, and became a costume designer. Such eclectic influences make for exciting apparel – rustic chic with a Japanese propensity for asymmetry.
225 Carral Street, T 604 633 9559, huntandgather.ca

Meinhardt Fine Foods

This emporium has become something of a South Granville institution in the decade since caterer Linda Meinhardt set up shop. It's still hard to find a place that smells, tastes or looks as good as this tried and true foodie destination. The local and foreign produce is a draw, as are the hard-to-find speciality items and the on-site florist. And now the deli counter isn't your only dine-in option, as the Peter Cardew-designed Picnic Café (T 604 732 4405) offers Meinhardt's delicacies next door. This sleek café was one of the first in town to introduce the concept of a single communal dining table, but the later addition of leather club chairs means the shy can now enjoy the *panini*, espresso and mouth-watering desserts too. *3002 Granville Street, T 604 732 4405, meinhardt.com*

Inform Interiors

Since the 1970s, when Niels and Nancy Bendtsen opened the first incarnation of what would become Inform Interiors, the couple have set the standard as designers and retailers of high-end modern furniture. Their 2,137 sq m Gastown store opened in 2006, created by young Vancouver designer Omer Arbel. It's essentially a big, elegantly proportioned box, punctuated by a large staircase, with a 15m skylight running above – you can stand on the roof garden and peer through it to the bottom floor. Locals come here to buy B&B Italia, Bocci lighting, Inform's own line of Bensen furniture – designed by Niels – and homewares by Vancouver favourite Molo.
50 Water Street, T 604 682 3868, informinteriors.com

Peking Lounge

Imagine one of those magical Chinatown emporiums in a film noir. Now visualise it with a design-friendly edge and a touch of Maoist tongue-in-cheek chic and you have a good picture of Peking Lounge. Launched in 2003 by Michael Bennett and Daniel Poulin, who fell in love with Chinese antiques during a stint in Beijing, Peking Lounge was a pioneer on this once-troubled block of E Pender Street. Located at the heart of contemporary Chinatown, it's set next to real-estate marketeer Bob Rennie's new condos but only minutes away from the infamous Main and Hastings intersection. Among the antique armoires and smaller repurposed pieces, must-buys include Peking Lounge's own line of silk and linen cushions and porcelain by Spin. *83 E Pender Street, T 604 844 1559, pekinglounge.com*

The Silk Project

Artist, designer and academic Joanna Staniszkis has long been enamoured of natural fibres. Her epic Linen Project explored everything from the former mills of her native Poland to the life cycle of the flax plant itself, via art installations and fashion design. Her latest obsession, silk, has engendered a new retail space housed on South Granville's gallery row. Staniszkis travels the world to source fine, handwoven silks, linens and rare speciality wools, which she hand-dyes, prints and pleats. The results are one-off pieces whose rich colours and textures turn them into walking art.
1541 W 6th Avenue, T 604 732 3314, thesilkproject.com

John Fluevog
This new shoe palace in Gastown has a
slightly retro feel – and not only because
John Fluevog's footwear is bound to
induce nostalgia in fashion-conscious
Generation X-ers. The 465 sq m, atrium-
like space was once a parking lot and then
a Richard Kidd store, and is located
around the corner from Fluevog's original
shop – opened in the early 1970s with
his former partner Peter Fox. Fluevog's
homecoming fits nicely with Gastown's
renaissance, and a neighbourhood energy
last seen circa 1983. An upstairs level
functions as a design workshop and offers
an impressive view of the industrial
waterfront. On the main floor, shoppers
can lounge on leather furniture designed
by Fluevog, while vegetarians are catered
for with the Veggie Vogs shoe collection.
65 Water Street, T 604 688 6228,
fluevog.com

Obakki

One of Vancouver's most beautifully designed retail spaces is owned and managed by Treana Peake, the wife of Nickelback guitarist Ryan. Raw concrete walls contrast with polished concrete floors, Corian meets reclaimed spruce, and a wash of light pours over exposed brick in local architects MGB's 511 sq m space. Menswear and womenswear collections come in a spare palette and are made locally – Obakki functions as a design collective, overseen by Peake. In some ways these are clothes for grown-up grungers, ready for clean, modern classics with a hint of rock'n'roll attitude. *44 Water Street, T 604 669 9727, obakki.com*

SPORTS AND SPAS
WORK OUT, CHILL OUT OR JUST WATCH

A mild climate and stunning surrounds make Vancouver ideal for an outdoor workout. Thousands of locals walk, run, cycle, hike, ski, inline skate or kayak around the city's perimeters. There's even something that Vancouverites do for fun called the Grouse Grind, which is a challenging, 2.9km, almost vertical climb to the summit of Grouse Mountain. There are less dramatic options. Hollyburn Lodge (opposite) is a charming spot where you can retreat for a hot chocolate after a day of snow-shoeing or cross-country skiing. And no winter-sports fan should leave Canada without catching at least one game of ice hockey, the favourite national spectator sport. You can see Vancouver's home team, the Canucks, play at General Motors Place (800 Griffiths Way, T 604 899 4600).

If it is too chilly to exercise outside, good gym options are the Sunset Community Centre (overleaf), designed by Bing Thom, where you can take part in numerous activities and admire the architecture, and Noam Gagnon's Wellness Center (see p092), a similarly sleek, well-designed space that specialises in Pilates. If you are a swimmer, and in town in the summer, head to the outdoor Kits Pool (see p094), open mid-May to mid-September. Post-workout, the city's best spa experiences are to be found at the Miraj Hammam Spa (1495 W 6th Avenue, T 604 733 5151) and the slick Spruce Body Lab (1128 Richards Street, T 604 683 3220). *For full addresses, see Resources.*

Hollyburn Lodge

Set up as a ski camp by local Scandinavian families in 1926, this lodge on Cypress Mountain was once accessible only via ski lift. After the Cypress Bowl Road was b   in 1975, it was discovered by a whole new generation of cross-country skiers. Thankfully, the timber-frame lodge, with its pitched metal roof and wood-burning stove, has maintained its original charm and still offers a peaceful escape from the flashy, noisy downhill scene in the nearby Cypress Bowl ski area, which will host the snowboard and freestyle skiing events a the 2010 Winter Olympics. You can drive or catch a bus to this area, which is half an h   from Downtown, then hike, snowshoe or ski to the lodge. Fondue nights and m   evenings here are winter highlights. *Top of Cypress Bowl Road, T 604 926 5612, cypressmountain.com*

Sunset Community Centre

Located near the heart of Vancouver's Punjabi market, Bing Thom's Sunset Community Centre is built on quite a foundation. The original centre, located two blocks west, was opened in 1947, after the president of the local community association asked another Bing, legendary crooner Crosby, to fly out and perform at a fund-raising benefit. Miraculously, he agreed. Bing Thom's new building is formed from concrete, glass and wood, and features a fluid, sculptural roof. Based on sustainable design principles, it's a light, airy space, in which the various sections pull off a central ramp. You can work out in the gym (a day pass costs around £2.60) or attend drop-in classes, from karate to belly dancing (from £6). *6810 Main Street, T 604 718 6505, mysunset.net*

Noam Gagnon's Wellness Center
Designed by local architect Noel Best,
this stylish studio was once a humdrum
office building. Now, a subtle interplay
of light and shade, achieved via the use
of sheer curtains and fluorescent panels,
has transformed the space. Gagnon's
years of experience as both a dancer
and a teacher make for expert classes.
*928 Davie Street, T 604 684 9711,
beyondpilatesvancouver.com*

Kits Pool

Built in the 1930s as a heated alternative to swimming in the open sea, this 137m filtered saltwater pool arcs out slightly to embrace its ocean border. Insiders know that the best time to swim here is in late May, after the Victoria Day weekend that marks the start of summer. This is also when the saltwater level peaks, meaning you receive a virtual thalassotherapy session as you swim. A serious lane area allows you to experience the full length of the pool while gazing out towards English Bay. Kits pool is also a favourite venue of triathletes, and you'll notice a few wetsuits early in the season, though most locals tough it out in swimwear. On a hot, sunny day, this is a great place to lounge and people-watch. When the pool closes in mid-September, it reverts to a somewhat wilder state, with ducks, gulls and herons taking up residence.
2305 Cornwall Avenue, T 604 731 0011

ESCAPES

WHERE TO GO IF YOU WANT TO LEAVE TOWN

While many would consider Lotusland an escape in itself, it's good to leave the big-city traffic, density and noise behind sometimes. Luckily, trip options are bountiful, and wilderness can be found only 45 minutes from town. Some destinations are more remote than others, but happily, as ecotourism surges in popularity, so does the demand for concomitant luxe linens and fine dining.

The wild and the civilised exist in perfect harmony at the Rockwater Secret Cove Resort (see p102) on the Sunshine Coast. Here, you can stay cocooned in condominium-style tents that are perched among the trees or on seaside rocks. Similarly, the Wickaninnish Inn (500 Osprey Lane, Tofino, T 250 725 3100), on the west coast of Vancouver Island, offers Relais & Chateaux-style luxury in a UNESCO biosphere reserve. Meanwhile, the Echo Valley Ranch and Spa (Jesmond Road, Clinton, T 250 459 2386) offers a surreal blend of Thai culture and architecture, and dude ranch, deep in the heart of British Columbia's cowboy country.

Those who want some witty design with their skiing should make for Whistler's Adara Hotel (see p100), a retro-camp take on the traditional lodge, while on a more serious architectural note, Erickson fans should decamp to Baldwin House (overleaf). Oenophiles will be thrilled to learn that the stunning Mission Hill Winery (opposite), in the Okanagan Valley, now has a guesthouse. *For full addresses, see Resources.*

Mission Hill Winery, Okanagan Valley

Okanagan Valley's ideal wine-growing climate has made the area Canada's answer to Napa, but its growing economy and population has also resulted in some nasty mall-style sprawl. Happily, Anthony Von Mandl's Mission Hill Winery, conceived by the Seattle-based architect Tom Kundig, provides respite design- and wine-wise. Spend the day sampling Mission Hill's excellent wines, lunching at the Terrace restaurant, touring the underground cellar, which was blasted out of volcanic rock, or simply admiring the architecture and surrounding landscape. You can stay over at Mission Hill's guesthouse, The Lake House on Green Bay (T 250 768 8886), and in summer take in a concert or a play at the winery's grass amphitheatre.
*1730 Mission Hill Road, Westbank,
T 250 768 6448, missionhillwinery.com*

Baldwin House, Burnaby
For architourists, a near-perfect escape
lies just 30 minutes' drive from Downtown.
Arthur Erickson's Baldwin House, set on
the shores of Deer Lake, is available to
rent via The Land Conservancy of British
Columbia, a body similar to The National
Trust. The modernist post-and-beam
house was commissioned by Dr William
and Ruth Baldwin in 1963, on the heels
of Erickson's commission for Simon Fraser
University's Burnaby campus (see p070).
Built into a hillside, the house was partly
inspired by the architect's travels to India,
in particular to the houseboats of Kashmir.
The building was conceived as a pavilion,
and with its pared-down palette of glass
and wood, numerous balconies and
surrounding landscaping, including a
reflecting pool, Baldwin House achieves
an effortless indoor/outdoor aesthetic.
6543/6572 Deer Lake Drive,
T 250 383 4627, conservancy.bc.ca

Adara Hotel, Whistler

Though it will welcome the world's sporting élite in 2010, Whistler is the Stepford Wife of mountain resorts, with a soullessness that belies its natural beauty. Thankfully, for Olympians and keen skiers with delicate design sensibilities, there's an encouraging presence in the form of the Adara Hotel. In an unlikely corner of the 'village', above Buffalo Bill's, a bar favoured mostly by beer-loving snowboarders, Vancouver's Box Interior Design carved a 41-room boutique hotel out of an exsiting 1980s condo-style Timberline Hotel. Its playful ode to the mountain-chalet style – a kind of urban alpine look with a retro-glam feel, as in the lobby (right) – comes with references to its previous guise. The stuffed moose head, a hallmark of the Timberline, enjoys a position of faux-reverential prominence in the Penthouse Suite.
4122 Village Green, T 604 905 4009, adarahotel.ca

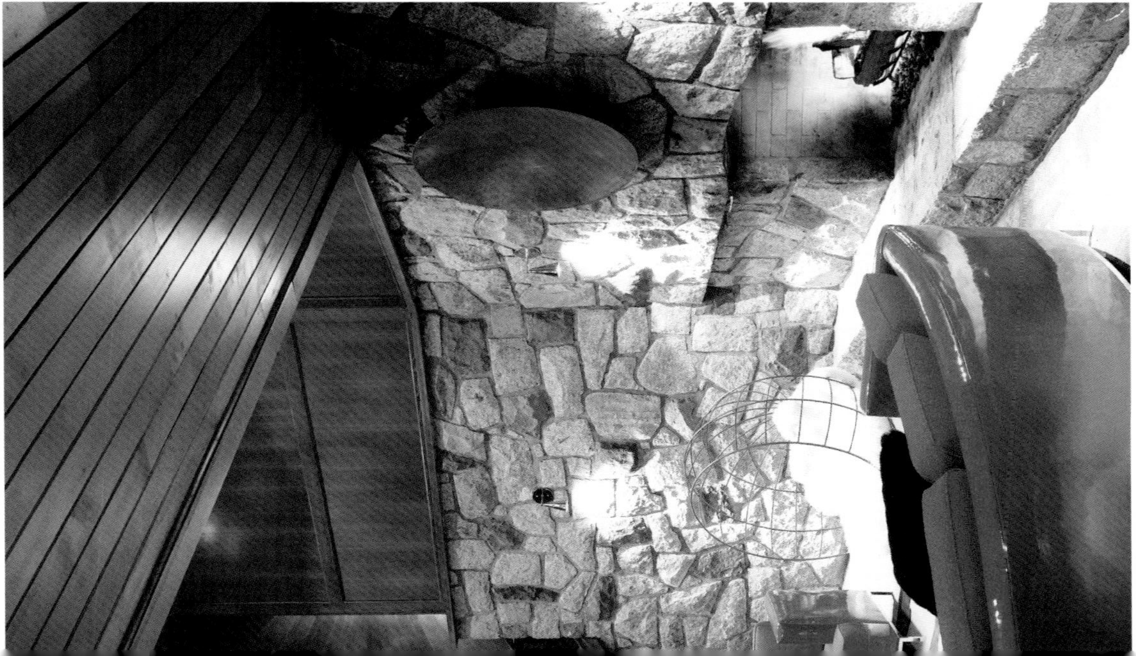

Rockwater Secret Cove Resort
Those who still dream of sleeping in
a treehouse should book one of Secret
Cove's 13 Tenthouse Suites. Poised high
up among the Arbutus trees, these mini-
pods are havens of tranquillity. You need
only emerge occasionally for a massage
and chef Steven Ewing's delicious fare.
*5356 Ole's Cove Road, Halfmoon Bay,
T 604 885 7038,
rockwatersecretcoveresort.com*

NOTES
SKETCHES AND MEMOS

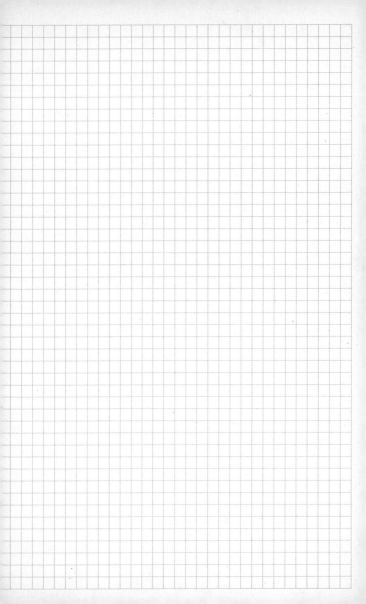

RESOURCES

CITY GUIDE DIRECTORY

HOTELS
ADDRESSES AND ROOM RATES

Adara Hotel 100
  Room rates:
  double, C$285;
  Penthouse Suite, C$470
  4122 Village Green
  Whistler
  T 604 905 4009
  adarahotel.ca
Baldwin House 098
  Room rates:
  house rental, from C$275
  6543/6572 Deer Lake Drive
  Burnaby
  T 250 383 4627
  conservancy.bc.ca
Echo Valley Ranch and Spa 096
  Room rates:
  double, C$600
  Jesmond Road
  Clinton
  T 250 459 2386
  evranch.com
The Fairmont Hotel Vancouver 026
  Room rates:
  double, from C$340;
  Gold Loggia Suite, from C$435
  900 W Georgia Street
  T 604 684 3131
  fairmont.com/hotelvancouver
Four Seasons 016
  Room rates:
  double, from C$320
  791 W Georgia Street
  T 604 689 9333
  fourseasons.com/vancouver

Hotel Georgia 016
  Room rates:
  prices on request
  801 W Georgia Street
  T 604 682 8107
  residencesatgeorgia.com
Hyatt Regency 024
  Room rates:
  double, from C$260;
  Signature Suite 3304, C$2,875
  655 Burrard Street
  T 604 683 1234
  vancouver.hyatt.com
The Lake House on Green Bay 097
  Room rates:
  double, C$205
  1454 Green Bay Road
  Westbank
  Okanagan Valley
  T 250 768 8886
  lakehouseongreenbay.com
The Listel Hotel 022
  Room rates:
  double, from C$195
  1300 Robson Street
  T 604 684 8461
  thelistelhotel.com
Loden 030
  Room rates:
  Deluxe King, from C$460;
  Halo Penthouse, from C$3,450
  1177 Melville Street
  T 604 669 5060
  lodenvancouver.com

Moda Hotel 017
Room rates:
double, from C$115;
Deluxe King Suite 427, from C$205
900 Seymour Street
T 604 683 4251
modahotel.ca

Opus Hotel 018
Room rates:
double, from C$380;
Opus Penthouse, from C$970
322 Davie Street
T 604 642 6787
opushotel.com

Pacific Palisades 028
Room rates:
double, from C$155;
Rouge Over Robson Penthouse Suite,
from C$200
1277 Robson Street
T 604 688 0461
pacificpalisadeshotel.com

Pan Pacific 010
Room rates:
double, from C$470;
Opal Suite, from C$4,025
300-999 Canada Place
T 604 662 8111
vancouver.panpacific.com

Rockwater Secret Cove Resort 102
Room rates:
double, from C$140;
Tenthouse Suite, from C$250
5356 Ole's Cove Road
Halfmoon Bay
T 604 885 7038
rockwatersecretcoveresort.com

Shangri-La 009
Room rates:
double, from C$390
1128 W Georgia Street
T 604 689 1120
shangri-la.com

Wedgewood Hotel 016
Room rates:
double, from C$575;
Penthouse Suite, from C$1,035
845 Hornby Street
T 604 689 7777
wedgewoodhotel.com

The Westin Bayshore 019
Room rates:
double, C$575;
Howard Hughes Suite, C$920;
International Suite, C$5,750
1601 Bayshore Drive
T 604 682 3377
westinbayshore.com

Wickaninnish Inn 096
Room rates:
double, from C$280
500 Osprey Lane
Tofino
Vancouver Island
T 250 725 3100
wickinn.com

WALLPAPER* CITY GUIDES

Editorial Director
Richard Cook

Art Director
Loran Stosskopf
Editor
Rachael Moloney
Author
Hadani Ditmars
Deputy Editor
Jeremy Case
Managing Editor
Jessica Diamond

Chief Designer
Daniel Shrimpton
Designer
Lara Collins
Map Illustrator
Russell Bell

Photography Editor
Sophie Corben
Photography Assistant
Robin Key

Sub-Editors
Vicky McGinlay
Melanie Parr
Editorial Assistant
Ella Marshall

Intern
Karen Smith

**Wallpaper* Group
Editor-in-Chief**
Tony Chambers
Publishing Director
Gord Ray
Publisher
Neil Sumner

Contributors
Sara Henrichs
Meirion Pritchard
Ellie Stathaki

Wallpaper* ® is a
registered trademark
of IPC Media Limited

All prices are correct at
time of going to press,
but are subject to change.

PHAIDON

Phaidon Press Limited
Regent's Wharf
All Saints Street
London N1 9PA

Phaidon Press Inc
180 Varick Street
New York, NY 10014

Phaidon® is a registered
trademark of Phaidon
Press Limited

www.phaidon.com

First published 2008
© 2008 IPC Media Limited

ISBN 978 0 7148 4902 7

A CIP Catalogue record for
this book is available from
the British Library.

Printed in China

PHOTOGRAPHERS

Michael Boland
One Wall Centre, p012
BC Place, pp014-015
Moda Hotel, p017
Opus Hotel, p018
The Westin Bayshore,
p019, pp020-021
The Listel Hotel,
p022, p023
Hyatt Regency, p024, p025
The Fairmount Hotel,
p026, p027
Pacific Palisades,
p028, p029
Loden, pp030-031
Granville Island, p033
Morris and Helen Belkin
Art Gallery, p034
Museum of
Anthropology, p035
Raincity Grill, p036
Monte Clark Gallery, p037
Watermark, p038
George, p039
Tojo's, p041
Gastropod, p042
Epicurean Caffè, p043
Salt Tasting Room,
pp044-045
Havana, p046
Cobre, p047
Coast, p048
Six Acres, p049
Habit, pp050-051
Yew, p052

Aurora Bistro, p053
Blue Water Café + Raw
Bar, p054
West, p055
The Pear Tree, p056
Le Marrakech, p057
Sanafir, p058
Republic, p059
Vij's, p060
The Cellar Restaurant/
Jazz Club, p061
Jane Cox, p063
MacMillan Bloedel
Building, p068
Marine Building, p069
Hunt and Gather,
pp076-077
Meinhardt Fine Foods,
pp078-079
Inform Interiors,
pp080-081
Peking Lounge, p082
The Silk Project, p083
John Fluevog, pp084-085
Obakki, pp086-087
Hollyburn Lodge, p089
Kitsilano Pool, pp094-095

**The British Columbia
Collection/Alamy**
Vancouver city view,
inside front cover

**Scott Gilchrist/
Archivision**
Robson Square, p067

**Hemera Technologies/
Jupiter**
Canada Place, pp010-011

Derek Lepper
Robson Square, p066

Heather Skydt
Baldwin House, Burnaby,
pp098-099

Steven Zhen Wang
Simon Fraser University,
pp070-071

VANCOUVER
A COLOUR-CODED GUIDE TO THE HOT 'HOODS

KITSILANO
The real bohos have been forced out as laid-back Kits has turned into Venice Beach North

SOUTH GRANVILLE
Railway barons' mansions house Vancouver's wealthy, while boutiques and cafés abound

SOUTH MAIN
Quirky art enclave SoMa is moving upmarket as condos and fashion stores spring up

DOWNTOWN
Always buzzy, the densely populated business district is full of shops and restaurants

CHINATOWN
The second largest Chinatown in North America has great architecture and night markets

WEST END
After a 1980s retail hijack, this area is now young, vibrant and home to the city's gay village

GASTOWN
The historic buildings of the city's oldest 'hood now house edgy design studios and eateries

VALETOWN
Warehouses are now high-end condos surrounded by shopping and fine-dining venues

For a full description of each neighbourhood, see the Introduction.
Featured venues are colour-coded, according to the district in which they are located.